THE SOMERSET & DORSET

The Postwar Years

Adrian Kennedy

UNIQUE BOOKS

Front cover:
It is New Year's Day 1966 and the last year of operation of the lines of the Somerset & Dorset has just commenced as Ivatt-designed 2-6-2T No 41290 waits at Glastonbury with the 1.15pm service from Evercreech Junction.
Roy Hobbs/Online Transport Archive

Previous page:
The Somerset & Dorset had numerous photographic locations that became well-known to enthusiasts through the work of the railway photographers. One such site was the viaduct just to the south of Midford station where the long stretch of double track that reached as far as Templecombe commenced. Midford was also the point at which the 13-mile climb to Masbury started and, during July 1960, the crew of 'West Country' No 34012 *Lapford* face the gradient with a service from Nottingham to Bournemouth. *Derek Cross*

The Somerset & Dorset: The Postwar Years
Adrian Kennedy

First published in the United Kingdom by Unique Books 2022

ISBN: 978 1 913555 10 8

A CIP record for this book is available from the British Library

Unique Books is an imprint of Unique Publishing Services Ltd, 3 Merton Court, The Strand, Brighton Marina Village, Brighton BN2 5XY.

www.uniquebooks.pub

Printed in India

A note on the photographs
Most of the illustrations in this book have been drawn from the collection of the Online Transport Archive, a UK-registered charity that was set up to accommodate collections put together by transport enthusiasts who wished to see their precious images secured for the long-term. Further information about the archive can be found at:
www.onlinetransportarchive.org
or email secretary@onlinetransportarchive.org

INTRODUCTION

The genesis of the Somerset & Dorset Joint lay in two earlier railways — the Somerset Central and the Dorset Central — which had merged on 1 September 1862 to create the Somerset & Dorset Railway. At that date the newly amalgamated railway operated from Burnham through to Glastonbury and Templecombe along with the Wells branch and the separate section from Blandford to Wimborne. The line linking Templecombe with Blandford opened on 31 August 1863. Through the exercise of running powers over the London & South Western from Wimborne, where services had to reverse, Somerset & Dorset Railway services reached Poole.

Although latterly treated as a branch, the route from Glastonbury to Highbridge was, historically, the first section of the future Somerset & Dorset Joint to open. Incorporated by an Act of Parliament on 17 June 1852, the Somerset Central Railway was empowered to construct a broad-gage line from Glastonbury to the Bristol Channel at Highbridge Wharf. Backed by, but independent of, the Bristol & Exeter, the new railway was designed to provide a route for manufactured goods from Glastonbury to the sea for onward shipment. The B&ER had acquired the Glastonbury Canal and, with agreement, the new railway was partially constructed along the route of the canal. The line opened on 28 August 1854 and was operated by the B&ER. There were five stations – Glastonbury, Ashcott, Shapwick, Edington and Bason Bridge – although Ashcott, Edington and Bason Bridge didn't appear in timetables until 1856 – with services terminating at the B&ER's Highbridge station; there were also goods facilities at Highbridge Wharf, to the west of the B&ER station. Highbridge was selected as the line's terminus rather than Bridgwater as the terrain offered a less challenging route. The Somerset Central Railway was extended through the opening of lines to Burnham on 3 May 1858 and Wells on 15 March 1859; the only intermediate station on the line to Wells was that at Polsham which did not appear in the timetable until 1861 although was probably extant from the line's opening. Both of the extensions were constructed as broad-gauge lines and operation by the B&ER continued until 1862 when the lines were converted to standard gauge.

The second key railway in the development of the Somerset & Dorset was the Dorset Central Railway. This was incorporated on 29 July 1856 and opened between Wimborne and Blandford on 1 November 1860. The line was built to standard gauge and was operated from opening by the London & South Western and there were two intermediate stations — Spetisbury and Sturminster Marshall — that opened with the line; the latter was renamed Bailey Gate in 1863.

The impetus to head north towards Bath came with the opening of the Midland Railway's line to Bath, which had been completed in 1869, and the access that a northern extension would offer to the railway in terms of exploiting part of the North Somerset coalfield. The line from Evercreech Junction to Bath, which is the primary subject of this volume, was authorised by an Act of Parliament on 21 August 1871 and was opened throughout on 20 July 1874. At Bath, the Somerset & Dorset Railway was granted running powers over half a mile of line into the Midland Railway's Bath station. The station was known as 'Queens Square' but this suffix was dropped during World War 2; it became Bath Green Park on 18 June 1951, following Nationalisation of the railways three years earlier.

The section of line north from Evercreech Junction was more demanding than the southern section, resulting in the construction of several tunnels and notable viaducts. At its maximum, the line included gradients of 1 in 50 as well as a summit at 811ft above sea level. Although built surprisingly quickly, given the engineering challenges, the cost of the route was such that it fundamentally undermined the finances of the Somerset & Dorset Railway; indeed such was the parlous state of the company's finances that the contractor actually ceased work on the northern extension for a brief period. Having invested in the extension, the railway now required support; although having been backed by the Bristol & Exeter originally it might have been likely that the Great Western was an obvious suitor, given that the B&ER and GWR were already negotiating a merger, and indeed the S&DR approached the GWR with a view to a takeover. However, the larger company handled the possible deal in a way that alienated the S&DR with the result that negotiations commenced with the London & South Western and Midland railways. On 1 November 1875 the S&DR signed a 999-year lease with the LSWR and MR, with the transfer obtaining parliamentary approval, despite the opposition of the GWR, on 13 July 1876.

The final section of the Somerset & Dorset to open was the line from Edington Road — later renamed Edington Junction — to Bridgwater. The independent Bridgewater [sic] Railway opened its seven-mile line on 21 July 1890 having been authorised to construct the line by Act of Parliament on 18 August 1882. At the time of opening there was one intermediate station – Cossington – but a second – Bawdrip Halt – opened on 9 July 1923. The line was operated by the S&DJR as part of a working arrangement that the smaller company had with the LSWR; at the Grouping in 1923 ownership of the line passed to the Southern.

From the mid-1880s onwards sections of the main line were doubled to increase capacity; in terms of the route from Evercreech Junction to Broadstone, the line remained single track from Templecombe through to Blandford, with passing loops at Stalbridge and Shillingstone, and from Corfe Mullen to Creekmoor Junction.

With the Grouping of the railways from 1 January 1923, the Somerset & Dorset passed to the control of the LMS and Southern railways. By this date the section of line from Corfe Mullen Junction through to Wimborne had already lost its passenger services – on 11 July 1920 – but remained opened for freight traffic only. The section between Carter's Siding and Wimborne was, however, to close completely on 17 June 1933.

Nationalisation came on 1 January 1948 when, along with the rest of the lines owned and operated by the LMS and Southern, the Somerset & Dorset Joint passed to the newly created British Transport Commission. Initially management of the route was handled by the Southern Region but, in 1958, operation of the line north of Templecombe passed to the Western Region. This was the start of a five-year period in which many of the through services, such as the famous 'Pines Express', were diverted away from the Somerset & Dorset as the inexorable run down of the line towards final closure progressed. The line's death sentence was effectively announced by Dr Richard Beeching in March 1963 with the publication of his report *The Reshaping of British Railways*. Both the main line from Bournemouth to Bath, along with the associated ex-Midland line, and the branch to Highbridge were listed for closure. There were those that campaigned against closure, such as the future Poet Laureate John Betjeman (who made an impassioned plea for the line's retention in a BBC documentary called *Branch Line Railway*), but these appeals came to nothing.

Closure of certain sections of the Somerset & Dorset had started relatively early. The branch from Glastonbury & Street to Wells was to lose its passenger service and close completely on 29 October 1951; the same day saw the withdrawal of scheduled passenger services on the extension from Highbridge to Burnham on Sea (although specials continued to operate over the extension until 1962). This was followed on 1 December 1952 by the

To **BRISTOL**

BATH GREEN PARK

MIDFORD

WELLOW

RADSTOCK · SHOSCOMBE & SINGLE HILL

CHILCOMPTON · MIDSOMER NORTON

BINEGAR

BURNHAM ON SEA

HIGHBRIDGE · BASON BRIDGE · To **YATTON**

EDINGTON BURTLE · WELLS · MASBURY

COSSINGTON · SHAPWICK · SHEPTON MALLET

BAWDRIP · POLSHAM

ASHCOTT · PYLLE

BRIDGWATER · GLASTONBURY & STREET · WEST PENNARD · EVERCREECH

EVERCREECH JUNCTION

COLE

WINCANTON

TEMPLECOMBE · To **SALISBURY**

To **EXETER** · HENSTRIDGE

STALBRIDGE

STURMINSTER NEWTON

SHILLINGSTONE · STOURPAINE & DURWESTON

BLANDFORD FORUM · CHARLTON MARSHALL

SPETISBURY · To **BROCKENHURST**

BAILEY GATE · WIMBORNE

CORFE MULLEN · BROADSTONE JUNCTION

BOURNEMOUTH CENTRAL

To **WEYMOUTH** · To **SOUTHAMPTON**

BOURNEMOUTH WEST

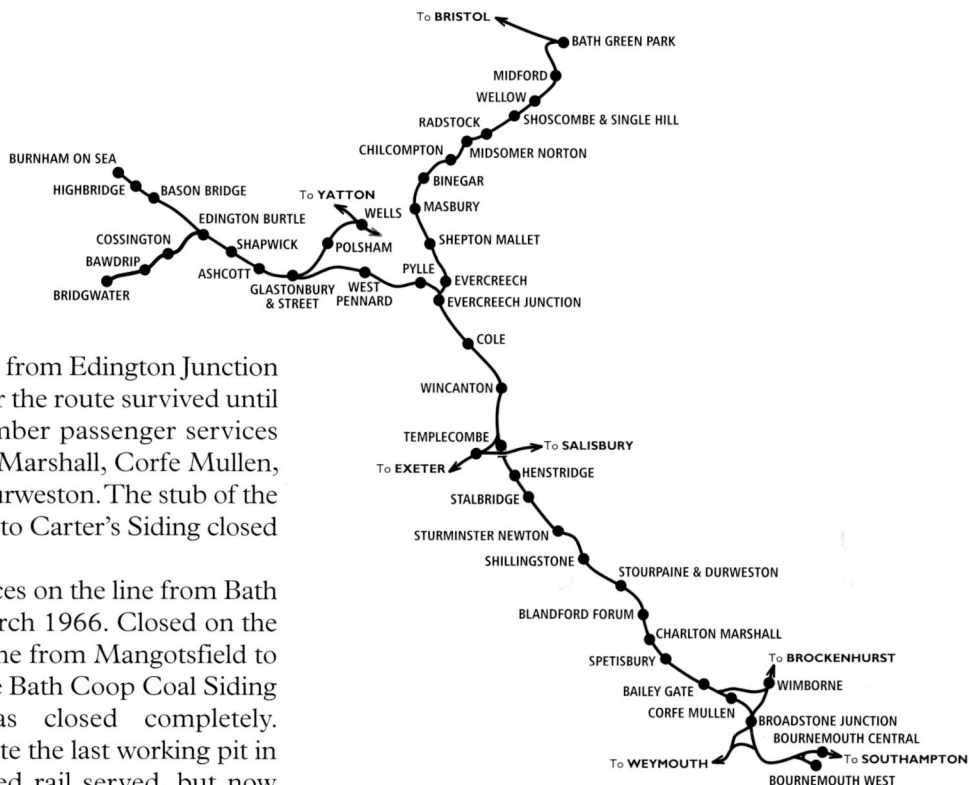

withdrawal of passenger services from Edington Junction to Bridgwater; freight traffic over the route survived until 1 October 1954. On 17 September passenger services were withdrawn from Charlton Marshall, Corfe Mullen, Spetisbury and Stourpaine & Durweston. The stub of the line from Corfe Mullen Junction to Carter's Siding closed on 19 September 1959.

The end of passenger services on the line from Bath to Bournemouth came on 7 March 1966. Closed on the same day was the ex-Midland line from Mangotsfield to Bath. The section south from the Bath Coop Coal Siding to Writhlington Colliery was closed completely. Writhlington Colliery, by this date the last working pit in the Radstock coalfield, remained rail served, but now access from a spur opened from the ex-Great Western line at Radstock; this short section of the erstwhile Somerset & Dorset remained open until 19 November 1973 and the closure of the colliery. The section from Bath Junction to serve the Bath Coop Coal siding remained open until 30 November 1967 and the ex-Midland route from Yate remained open for freight traffic until 31 May 1971. Part of the latter route is now preserved as the Avon Valley Railway. With the closure to passenger services, the sections from Evercreech Junction to the United Dairies Siding at Bason Bridge, from Templecombe No 3 Junction to Templecombe Lower and from Templecombe Junction to Templecombe were closed completely. After the closure, there remained two short sections of line open for freight traffic: Bason Bridge to Highbridge, for milk traffic, and Blandford to Broadstone for milk and freight. These sections of line closed on 2 October 1972 (except for a brief reprieve at the northern end for use of flyash trains during the construction of the M5) and 6 January 1969 respectively.

Freight traffic over the southern section of the main line were withdrawn between Blandford and Wincanton on 14 June 1965 and between Radstock and Wincanton on 3 January 1966 with the exception of coal traffic to Midsomer Norton that survived until 19 February 1966. Bournemouth West terminus was closed on 4 October 1965 with the result that passenger services were diverted to Bournemouth Central for the last few months of the line's existence.

The northern terminus of the Somerset & Dorset was at Bath Green Park where Class 4F No 44422 is seen during 1960. The station, which was designed by the Midland Railway's architect John Holloway Sanders, opened on 7 May 1870 as the terminus of the MR's line from line from Mangotsfield. The Somerset & Dorset arrived in Bath four years later and exercised running powers over the MR to reach the two-platform station. In April 1942 the station's overall roof suffered some damage as a result of Luftwaffe bombing during the 'Baedeker Raids'; these attacks – launched against five culturally important cities (Canterbury, Exeter, Norwich and York were also attacked) – were a response to the RAF's destruction of the German city of Lübeck. The damage was not repaired after the war. Closure of the station came with the withdrawal of passenger services over the line to Bournemouth in March 1966. The station – now Grade II listed – survives, however, and is now used for a variety of commercial activities. Another survivor is No 44422; withdrawn in June 1965, it was sold to the famous Woodham Bros scrapyard at Barry from where it was rescued in 1977. The locomotive was restored to operational condition on the Churnet Valley Railway and restoration was completed in 1992.
Les Folkard/Online Transport Archive

The damage wrought by the Luftwaffe during World War 2 is all too evident in this view of Class 7F No 53807 and Class 4F No 44558 awaiting departure from Green Park station on 6 June 1964 with a service to Templecombe. By this date the number of the ex-S&D 2-8-0s in service had been significantly reduced; at the start of 1964 only four of the class remained in service but, with the withdrawal of No 53809 in early June 1964, only No 53807 remained operational. The sole survivor battled on for a further four months until withdrawal in October 1964. Nos 53806-10 were built at Robert Stephenson & Hawthorns Ltd during 1925 – more than a decade after the original six locomotives had been constructed at Derby – and were fitted with slightly larger diameter boilers and left-hand drive. All had been fitted with smaller diameter boilers by 1955.
Derek Cross

One of the rare sights at Bath Green Park during the final obsequies of the S&D on Sunday 6 March 1966 was the presence of a DMU stabled in the station. The SLS (Midland Area) organised a special – promoted as the last train on the Somerset & Dorset line – that was steam-hauled both to and from Bournemouth West; however, a connecting service from Birmingham New Street, calling at Cheltenham Spa Lansdown and Gloucester Eastgate, was provided by a DMU. The unit was timetabled to arrive at 10.25am and depart at 6.25pm. Late running of the return from Bournemouth – it did not reach Bath until 6.51pm – will have resulted in the DMU's delayed departure. Travel by the DMU was restricted and required ownership of a ticket and itinerary for the onward service.
Gavin Morrison

The southbound 'Pines Express' is pictured departing from Bath Green Park on 9 September 1961 behind Standard Class 4MT No 75023 and 'West Country' No 34041 *Wilton*. When recorded here, the Standard 4-6-0 was a relatively recent arrival on the line; it had only been transferred from Gloucester Barnwood to Templecombe in the four-week period up to 7 October 1961 and was destined to be based on the line for a relatively brief period, being transferred to Machynlleth by early October the following year.
Gavin Morrison

The shed complex that eventually served Bath Green Park comprised two distinct buildings, situated to the north and the south of the coaling stage illustrated here. To the south – and out of view – was the original Midland Railway shed; this two-road stone-built shed was opened on 4 May 1869 but was latterly used solely for repair work prior to closure. The main running shed originally comprised a two-road wooden-built structure opened with the Somerset & Dorset Railway line on 20 July 1874. The shed was enlarged into a four-road structure four years later but the shed as illustrated here was the result of a further enlargement in 1884; this work also included the rearrangement of the shed yard and the improved coaling facilities. The turntable, situated to the right of where the photographer was standing to take this view, was enlarged from 46ft to 60ft in 1935. The complete shed, including the original MR structure, closed in March 1966.
R. W. A. Jones/Online Transport Archive

Pictured on shed at Bath Green Park is ex-S&D Class 7F 2-8-0 No 53809. The S&DJR had acquired – as a result of its part ownership by the Midland Railway – a number of standard MR designs for its locomotive stock; however, it was recognised that the line required more powerful locomotives to operate over the steeply-graded lines but no existing MR design fulfilled this requirement. As a result the MR's then CME, Henry Fowler, designed a specific class of 2-8-0; the first six – later BR Nos 53800-05 – were constructed at Derby Works between February and August 1914. After the Grouping, when the MR's co-ownership passed to the LMS, the new owners ordered a further batch of five – BR Nos 53806-10 – from Robert Stephenson & Hawthorns Ltd; these were built between July and August 1925. The later five differed from the original batch in being fitted with larger diameter boilers – later replaced with similar diameter boilers to the original five – and by being left-hand drive. The original batch were all withdrawn by February 1962 but the RSH quintet lasted longer, with the last not being withdrawn until October 1964. Two of the later batch – Nos 53808 and 53809 – were both sold to Woodham Bros for scrap and have subsequently both been preserved and restored.

R. W. A. Jones/Online Transport Archive

On 18 June 1963 BR Standard 4-6-0 No 75007 approaches Bath Junction with a service from Green Park to Templecombe. The junction marked the start of the 1 in 50 climb towards Combe Down Tunnel – a distance of about two miles. Although the S&D started from the junction as double track, it soon became single track for the ascent up Devonshire Bank with the drivers of Down trains picking up the single line token at Bath Junction. If a banking locomotive was required, the driver of this was given a separate token – the Bath bank engine staff – for its return journey to the junction. *Derek Cross*

Having departed from Bath Green Park and taken the S&D at Bath Junction, southbound services faced the gradient – a maximum of 1 in 50 – on the single-line section through Devonshire Tunnel to the first summit on the line at Combe Down. Pictured ascending the bank on 11 September 1958 with the 'Pines Express' are Class 2P No 40569 and Standard Class 5 No 73062. Although the precursor the service had operated through from Manchester in 1910, it was not until 26 September 1927 that the service was named the 'Pines Express'. It was the transfer of this major service to operate via Oxford, Reading and Basingstoke after it last operated over the S&D on 8 September 1962 that was an indication that the importance of the S&D was being reduced. *Alexander McBlain/Online Transport Archive*

In June 1960 the last of the Midland Railway-built Class 7Fs – No 53805 – is seen ascending Devonshire Bank with the Down coal empties destined for Midsomer Norton. Completed at Derby Works in August 1914 by the time the locomotive was recorded here it was approaching the end of its long career; it was withdrawn from Bath Green Park shed in March 1961. *Derek Cross*

In June 1959 Class 4F No 44096 and 'West Country' No 34041 *Wilton* emerge from the 447yd-long Devonshire Tunnel with a service from Bournemouth to Liverpool descends the 1 in 50 gradient towards Bath Green Park. Having been effectively closed up for many years, Devonshire and Combe Down tunnels were assessed during the summer of 2009 in order to ascertain their condition before work started during March 2010 to incorporate the two into a new footpath and cycleway linking Bath with the existing National Cycle Route 24 southwards to Midford. The Two Tunnels Greenway was completed in 2013. *Derek Cross*

Heading south, the first station that Bournemouth-bound trains would encounter was Midford. The small goods yard which served Midford was located to the north of the station and access to it was controlled by a small ground frame – Midford A (seen here on 12 August 1961 as Class 9F No 92000 heads south with a passenger service). The ground frame was released by the section tablet and provided access to the two short sidings provided. Freight traffic to MIdford ceased on 10 June 1963 and the connection was removed 12 months later.
R. C. Riley/Transport Treasury

Having just crossed Midford Viaduct, BR Standard 2-64T No 80032 enters the single platform at Midford station on 1 October 1965 with a service towards Bath. The tall latticed signal visible on the platform was a backing signal for use in the event of a train stalling on the steep gradient towards Combe Down. If there was a train failure, the driver made use of the phone adjacent to the tunnel for permission to set back to the station. With the signal pulled off, the train could then reverse on to the Up line of the viaduct to await assistance. The station and signalbox were demolished after closure but the platform and trackbed remained and were subsequently incorporated into the Two Tunnels Greenway. The station site has been purchased by the New Somerset & Dorset Railway with a view to its eventual restoration.
Derek Cross

Immediately south of Midford station and the start of the 32-mile section of double track through to Templecombe was the 168yd-long eight-arch Midford viaduct and, on 15 August 1961, BR Standard 4MT 2-6-0 No 76009 is recorded heading north into the station with a service from Bournemouth to Bristol. When the line from Templecombe to Bath was constructed, the alignment was single track only; however, in order to increase capacity, the route northwards from Templecombe was doubled and, in 1903, the viaduct at Midford was widened to accommodate a second running line; plans for the doubling through to Bath were abandoned of cost grounds. The original single-track viaduct is represented by the eastern half of the viaduct and so the northbound train is operating over the part constructed in the early 20th century. Since 2005 the viaduct has been incorporated within the Two Tunnels footpath and cycleway that makes use of the redundant trackbed as far as Wellow. *Derek Cross*

The approach to Wellow station from the south was through the Wellow Valley and its here that the northbound 'Pines Express' is pictured on 28 July 1952 with BR Standard 4 No 75009 piloting Class 9F 2-10-0 No 92210. The route of the S&D from Radstock to Midford followed closely the alignment of the earlier Radstock branch of the Somerset Coal Canal. When the branch was constructed during the first decade of the 19th century, it was planned to connect it to the canal's main line via a flight of locks. In the event this was never constructed and the branch was an isolated section linked to the rest of the network by a short tramway. This, allied to the lack of traffic on the branch, led to its closure and replacement by a tramway built on the towpath. This was the route when the Bath extension was constructed. *Derek Cross*

This is the view east from Radstock North towards Wellow and Bath on 31 May 1970. Visible is the stone-built two-road engine shed that was opened by the S&DJR in 1888 to replace an earlier one-road shed that had been opened by the original Somerset & Dorset Railway in 1874. The shed was closed on 7 March 1966 and, for a period thereafter, was occupied by the Somerset & Dorset Trust. The building was subsequently demolished. By this date, the section of the erstwhile S&D route from Radstock to Writhlington Colliery was accessed solely by the new connection completed in early 1966 from the ex-GWR Frome to Bristol line. Traffic over the connection to the colliery ceased on 19 November 1973. As with a number of other sections of the long-closed route, it is now virtually impossible to identify the route of the line at this point. *John Meredith/Online Transport Archive*

Known as simply Radstock until 26 September 1949, when the suffix 'North' was added to the station name, the S&D's station in the town opened on 20 July 1874. This undated view records Class 2P No 40564 and ex-S&D Class 7F 2-8-0 No 53810 heading eastbound through the station with a service towards Bath. The train has just passed Radstock North B box; this had originally been known as Radstock West but was renamed in 1951. The second box – Radstock East (North A until 1951) – was situated to the east of the station. Obscured by the train is the junction that had once existed to the west of the station; this provided access to the short branch that served Middle Pit (which closed in 1933) and Radstock gas works (closed 1950). The impressive building that forms the backdrop to this view is the now demolished Oak Hill brewery whilst the trackbed of the S&D line westwards to Midsomer Norton now forms the North Radstock Greenway.
Neville Stead Collection/Transport Treasury

The approach to Radstock in the Up direction meant crossing the level crossing the A367. Pictured arriving at the station in August 1958 is Class 2P 4-4-0 No 40563 piloting 'West Country' No 34108 *Wincanton* on a service from Bournemouth to Blackpool. After the Grouping in 1923 the MR 4-4-0 design of Johnson as rebuilt by Fowler was adopted as the company's new standard Class 2 locomotive; No 40563 was the first of 138 similar locomotives to be constructed at Derby (and later at Crewe) from March 1929 until December 1932. The new locomotives had driving wheels three inches smaller in diameter than the rebuilds and reduced diameter boilers albeit at a higher pressure. Allocated to Templecombe in the LMS's last month, December 1947, No 40563 was to spend the rest of its operational life there, being withdrawn in May 1962. Three of the type were supplied direct to the S&D in 1928; numbered 44-46 by the S&D, the trio became LMS Nos 633-35 in 1930 when the LMS absorbed the S&D's rolling stock.
Derek Cross

Located to the east of Midsomer Norton station was Norton Hill Colliery; this was one of the mines in the Somerset coalfield served by the S&D. The colliery was connected to the railway in 1900 with additional sidings being added later in the decade; these were reconstructed in the early 1950s. The seam here, however, was thin and the mine became increasingly uneconomic. Coal winding ceased on 11 February 1966 – just before the S&D closed – and the track was lifted. One of the locomotives employed by the National Coal Board, which had taken over the colliery from the Beauchamp family at Nationalisation, was this Hudswell Clarke 0-6-0ST. Built originally in 1913 (Works No 1029), the locomotive was rebuilt in 1931; when recorded here on 21 July 1950, the locomotive was approaching the end of its life. It was sold for scrap to C. Whitlock of Wapping Wharf, Bristol, in February 1951.
Tony Wickens/Online Transport Archive

Viewed looking towards the north on 17 September 1958, Class 3F 0-67-0T No 47557 stands light engine in front of Midsomer North South box. The station's main buildings were on the Down side and a small goods shed was also provided. The connection to Norton Hill Colliery was located immediately to the east of Bridge No 48 and can be seen ascending in the distance. Opened as Midsomer Norton with the line on 20 July 1874, the station was renamed Midsomer Norton & Welton on 16 October 1898 and became Midsomer Norton & Welton Upper on 26 September 1949 after Nationalisation in order to differentiate it from the neighbouring ex-GWR station. Freight facilities were withdrawn on 15 June 1964. The station at Midsomer Norton is leased by the Somerset & Dorset Railway Heritage Trust, which has restored the site and laid about a mile of track south towards Chilcompton. To the north, however, the road bridge over Silver Street has been demolished whilst any further extension southwards will require the removal of landfill and the restoration of the tunnel at Chilcompton. *Gavin Morrison*

During August 1961 Class 9F No 92212 has just passed through the short Chilcompton Tunnel with the 9.35am service from Sheffield to Bournemouth. When the 64-yard long tunnel was first completed in 1874, there was only a single bore – the future Down side; it was not until 1892, with the doubling of the line, that the second – Up – bore was completed. The tunnel is still extant and is now used by the Midsomer Norton Target Shooting Club. The '9F' is also a survivor. Less than two years old when recorded here – it was completed at Swindon Works in September 1959 – and a relatively recent arrival on the line – it had been transferred from Banbury to Bath Green Park in May/June 1961 – No 92212 was to survive until withdrawal in January 1968, having latterly been allocated to Carnforth. One of the class to be sold to Woodham Bros, it arrived at Barry in September 1968 and was rescued for preservation 11 years later. Restoration, undertaken at Loughborough on the Great Central Railway, was completed in September 1996.
Roy Hobbs/Online Transport Archive

Slightly to the north of Binegar were the sidings of the Mendip Stone Works and evidence of these sidings can be seen in the distance in this view of Class 4F 0-6-0 No 44422 heading southbound with a Down service passed the signalbox. Binegar station opened with the line on 20 July 1874; the station lost its freight facilities on 10 June 1963 and was to close completely with the withdrawal of passenger services over the S&D on 7 March 1966. The station was subsequently demolished and a new house built on the site. To the south of the Down platform was a building – later used as a goods shed – that was owned by the Oakhill Brewery; the company ran a 3ft 0in gauge line from the station eastwards to serve the at brewery at Oakhill itself – a distance of some two miles – from 1904 until 1921.
R. C. Riley/Transport Treasury

On 12 August 1961 Class 2P 4-4-0 No 40697 and 'West Country' No 34043 *Combe Martin* have almost just completed the 10-mile climb from Evercreech Junction as their Bournemouth to Manchester train enters Masbury station. The actual summit – 811ft – was located slightly to the north of the station. Masbury station, which had opened on 20 July 1874, was unstaffed from 26 September 1938. The box, which was in use when recorded here, was closed on 1 July 1964 at which stage the siding on the Up side to the south of the station were removed (freight facilities having been withdrawn on 10 June 1963). During World War 2 additional sidings had been added to the Down side south of the station in connection with a US Army camp; however; these were removed in 1959. The substantial station house at Masbury remains intact and is now in private ownership.
Neville Stead Collection/Transport Treasury

On 22 July 1961 Class 2P 4-4-0 No 40700 and BR Standard Class 5MT No 73019 have done the hard work as the train enters Masbury station from the north with a southbound service. The locomotive crews can now face the descent towards Evercreech Junction. Completed at Crewe Works in December 1932, the '2P' was allocated to Bath Green Park for its entire BR career, being withdrawn in August 1962. The '5MT' was to be based at Green Park for two periods during its relatively short life – between June 1958 and July 1960 and between October 1960 and April 1962 – before being based in Gloucester until transfer to the London Midland Region in early November 1964. It was withdrawn from Bolton shed in January 1967.
Les Folkard/Online Transport Archive

The twin Windsor Hill Tunnels are located to the south of Masbury and, on, 26 August 1961, Class 9F No 92212 emerges from the Down tunnel with a southbound service. The Down tunnel was the first to be constructed; the work in completing the 242yd-long structure was marked by tragedy when four navvies were killed and a fifth injured on 18 August 1873 when a block of stone fell from the roof. When the line was doubled in the early 1890s, a second bore – shorter at 132 yards – was constructed for Up services to the west of the existing bore. Following closure, the Down tunnel was used for a period by Rolls Royce for the testing of jet engines; this work required the insertion of steel doors but these were removed in 1991. The tunnels and trackbed remain largely intact on the 1 in 50 gradient past (and through) Windsor Hill. South of the tunnels were the sidings that served the Hamwood and Windsor Hill quarries.
Gavin Morrison

As the fireman works in the tender of Class 7F No 53807 on 26 August 1961, the train is almost ready to depart northwards from Shepton Mallet Charlton Road as the crew prepare themselves for the second stage of the ascent to the summit at Masbury. The station opened as Shepton Mallet on 20 July 1874 and had the suffix 'Charlton Road' added in about 1901.
Gavin Morrison

In June 1960 another of the ex-S&D Class 7Fs – No 53808 – is seen shunting the pick-up freight from Evercreech Junction to Bath at Shepton Mallet. In addition to the goods yard, situated on the Up side, there were sidings on the Down side that catered for a small quarry and associated stone crushing plant. Freight facilities were withdrawn from Shepton Mallet on 10 June 1963 and all of the sidings were out of use by the end of the following year. The station closed completely with the withdrawal of passenger services over the route on 7 March 1966. Since closure the station site at Shepton Mallet has been converted into an industrial estate although the 317yd-long Charlton Viaduct to the north of the station is still extant.
Derek Cross

On 30 June 1962, Class 9F No 92206 is seen departing from Shepton Mallet with a Down service from Bristol to Bournemouth. Visible on the platform in the background is the 26-lever signalbox that controlled the station. New in May 1959 and allocated to the Western Region when delivered from Swindon Works, No 92205 was transferred to Eastleigh at the start of January 1961 and would be based there until transferred to Feltham for three months in June 1963. The locomotive was then based at York and Wakefield until withdrawn in May 1967 – a working life of just over eight years. *Derek Cross*

South of Shepton Mallet the line passed through the cutting at Cannard's Grave and, on 30 June 1962 BR Standard Class 4 No 75073 and rebuilt 'West Country' No 34045 *Ottery St Mary* head north towards Shepton Mallet with an Up service from Bournemouth to Liverpool. Since the line's closure, this section of line has been completely infilled and the trackbed has been eliminated to a point just north of Prestleigh.
Derek Cross

Originally known as Evercreech when opened on 3 February 1862, the station was renamed Evercreech Junction on 20 July 1874 with the opening of the line through to Bath. The main station buildings – seen here from a northbound train on 7 January 1966 – were situated on the Down – southbound – platform. Freight facilities were withdrawn from Evercreech Junction on 29 November 1965 and the station closed completely on 7 March 1966. After some years of dereliction, the main station building and the two-storey stationmaster's house were both converted into private residences; they are both still extant as is the trackbed of the line south from the closed station. North of the station site, the goods yard, sidings and trackbed have been incorporated into an industrial estate.
John Meredith/Online Transport Archive

Ex-MR Class 1P 0-4-4T No 58072 stands in the Up platform at Evercreech Junction with the branch service towards Highbridge. The centre road visible in the view was a long siding; this terminated midway along the platform and was provided with an unusual buffer stop. This was fitted with a three-link coupling to which stabled stock was attached and was designed to prevent the stock rolling away down the 1 in 100 gradient towards the junction itself. No 58072 was originally built, to a design of Samuel Johnson for the Midland Railway, by Neilson, Reid & Co; new in September 1893, the locomotive was one of the type equipped with condensing apparatus for use through the tunnels on the Metropolitan line when operating London suburban services. It remained allocated to sheds in the London area until the late summer of 1950. Although the photograph is undated, it probably was taken during the summer of 1952 as the locomotive was reallocated to Highbridge shed by the middle of March that year. No 58072 was to remain based there until final withdrawal came in October 1956.
R. W. A. Jones/Online Transport Archive

On 16 August 1961 Class 2P 4-4-0 No 40700 arrives at Cole with a service from Evercreech Junction to Templecombe. Originally opened by the Dorset Central Railway on 3 February 1862 it was at Cole that the end-on junction with the Somerset Central Railway to Glastonbury & Street was made; this link was also opened on 3 February 1862. The station was provided with two platforms and a small goods shed with cattle docks; freight facilities were, however, withdrawn from the station on 5 April 1965. The small 14-frame signalbox that was situated at the southern end of the Up platform is obscured by the arriving train; the box closed on 31 May 1965. The main station building, constructed in stone, was situated on the Down platform; this building is still extant, having been converted for residential use.
Derek Cross

South of Cole the line ascended again, but with gradients much less severe than those encountered on the climb to Masbury, as it approached Wincanton passed the village of Shepton Montague.

Pictured climbing towards Wincanton on 30 June 1962 is Class 4F No 44558 with a service from Bath to Templecombe. *Derek Cross*

The last of the ex-S&D Class 7F 2-18-0s – No 53810 – heads south at Wincanton on 16 July 1961 having just departed from the much shorter (80yd as opposed to the 150yd long Up) Down platform. Visible on the Up platform is the 14-lever signalbox. The station opened on 3 February 1862. The goods yard was used for bringing horses to and from the local racecourse whilst the facilities were further enhanced in 1933 by the construction of a siding to serve the Cow & Gate milk depot. Although general freight facilities were withdrawn from the station on 5 April 1965, milk traffic continued until the line's final closure. Today, although the trackbed of the line is still identifiable to the south of the A303 Wincanton bypass, the line through the town itself has largely disappeared with the station site itself redeveloped for commercial purposes. As is true of many of the communities once served by the S&D, Wincanton has grown significantly in the years since the S&D closed. *R. C. Riley/Transport Treasury*

On 30 December 1965 the second of the BR Standard Class 5 4-6-0s – No 73001 – is seen ascending the double track spur track, from Templecombe No 2 Junction, that linked the S&D line with Templecombe station. Since the line's closure, this area has been substantiall altered; the site of the junction and shed have been redeveloped for commercial purposes and the alignment of the spur has been incorporated into a road to provide access. *Gavin Morrison*

On 7 January 1966 BR Standard 4-6-0 75069 is seen standing outside the two-road shed at Templecombe. The first shed here was a small one-road timber-built structure constructed by the S&D and opened on 31 August 1863; this was replaced in 1877 by a larger two-road shed, again constructed in timber, but by Nationalisation this shed was in a poor condition and the shed illustrated here was constructed in 1951. The building was constructed in brick and concrete with a steel-framed asbestos roof. When illustrated here, it was approaching the end of its operational career as it closed, with the line, in March 1966. Following closure, the building was reused for commercial purposes until its demolition in 1997. The line curving to the east under the road bridge once formed a connection with the London & South Western main line towards Salisbury; this, however, was severed in 1870 and the stub of the line was used as a siding thereafter. *John Meredith/Online Transport Archive*

Having regained the S&D line No 73001 – with a crudely painted number rather than its smokebox plate – heads south through the platform at Templecombe Lower on 30 December 1965. The original S&D station at Templecombe, opened on 3 February 1862, was located to the north and was relocated to this site on 17 January 1887. The platform was not generally used – for example just prior to the outbreak of World War 2 only one train made use of it (an evening service from Bournemouth that terminated at it at 8.38pm) – but it remained notionally open until 3 January 1966. *Gavin Morrison*

There is already evidence of rationalisation at Henstridge on a dismal 1 January 1966 as 'Merchant Navy' No 35011 *General Steam Navigation* heads northwards with the LCGB 'Mendip Merchantman' special from Waterloo. This was the first occasion on which a 'Merchant Navy' had been permitted to operate over the S&D; prior to the tour, the class had been barred from the route as a result of weight restrictions. At the time the train was recorded it was running about 15 minutes late; things got worse as the day progressed and it was more than an hour late when it finally arrive back at Waterloo at 9.15pm. Henstridge was the smallest station on the line – with a platform of only 50 yards in length – and a single siding for freight; freight facilities were withdrawn on 5 April 1965 and, as can be seen, the track had been quickly lifted. Although the road overbridge to the north of the station is still extant and the trackbed through the site identifiable, the station itself has been demolished and the land to the west of the railway used for housing.
Derek Cross

It is 28 December 1965 and the S&D has witnessed its final Christmas as BR Standard 2-6-4T No 80039 stands awaiting departure from Stalbridge station with the 12 noon service from Templecombe to Bournemouth. By the date of the photograph the facilities at the station had already been reduced with the goods yard having closed on 5 April 1965 and the sidings being taken out of use on 7 July 1965. The signalbox, which also controlled the level crossing, remained operational until the closure of the line on 7 March 1966. The site of the station, which had a passing loop and two platforms, has been completely redeveloped for commercial purposes.

Gavin Morrison

Pictured approaching the 16-lever signalbox and the Up platform at Sturminster Newton on 4 July 1961 with a northbound service is Class 9F No 92001. The station opened on 31 August 1863. Sturminster Newton was another of the stations on the line where milk represented a significant source of traffic with a siding serving a factory on the Down side. Freight facilities were withdrawn from the station on 5 April 1965. Although the trackbed to the west and the east of the town – the latter now part of the North Dorset Trailway towards Shillingstone – survive, the route through the town itself has largely disappeared, to be replaced by gardens and, on the site of the station itself, a car park.
R. C. Riley/Transport Treasury

On 30 December 1965, BR Standard 2-6-4T No 80043 departs from Shillingstone with a northbound service. Again rationalisation is evident as the track serving the goods yard – freight facilities having been withdrawn on 5 April 1965 – has already been lifted. The trackbed passed the station has been incorporated into the North Dorset Trailway – the council's plans to use it as the basis of a Stillingstone bypass having been abandoned in 2002 – but the station itself, after having been in commercial hands, is now occupied by the North Dorset Railway, which has restored the surviving buildings and rebuilt those that had been demolished like the signalbox, and at the time of writing is extending its running line north towards Bere Marsh as part of its long term ambition to restore the line to Sturminster Newton. *Gavin Morrison*

Pictured taking water at Blandford Forum with a northbound service on 17 September 1964 is Ivatt-designed 2-6-2T No 41214. The original station serving the town was a temporary terminus – Blandford St Mary – situated to the south of the River Stour that opened on 1 November 1860. This was replaced by the station illustrated here, about 1½ miles further north, on 31 August 1863. The 27-lever signalbox on the Down platform was constructed to replace the original box, which had been constructed on the Up platform in 1893 but which had been destroyed by fire in 1906, when the line southwards to Corfe Mullen was doubled. To the south of the station was a branch that once served Blandford army camp; this was, however, short-lived, being opened on 12 January 1919 and being out of use two years later. Following the withdrawal of through passenger services on 7 March 1966, the line north of Blandford Forum was closed completely. Goods traffic, however, continued to operate from Broadstone to Blandford Forum until 6 January 1969 when freight facilities were withdrawn from the station. Following complete closure the station site was redeveloped as a housing estate.
Gavin Morrison

Viewed looking towards the north on 30 December 1965, BR Standard 2-6-4T No 80041 is seen arriving with a service towards Bournemouth at Bailey Gate. The station here opened as Sturminster Marshall on 1 November 1860 and was renamed in 1863. To the east of the station was a United Dairies milk and cheese plant; this provided a considerable amount of traffic from the station. Until 1933 this was routed via Wimborne; thereafter, until the line's closure, the traffic was routed via Templecombe. The section from Blandford Forum to Broadstone was retained until 6 January 1969 to cater for the remaining milk traffic and freight from Blandford Forum; general freight facilities were withdrawn from the station on 5 April 1965. Since closure the site has been redeveloped for commercial purposes and is now known as the Bailey Gate Industrial Estate. *Gavin Morrison*

Demonstrating the joint nature of the S&D LMS Class 5 No 5440 is seen at Bournemouth West during 1947, the last summer before the railways were Nationalised. The station opened on 15 June 1874; closure came on 6 September 1965 when all surviving services were transferred to terminate at Bournemouth Central (services over the S&D had been transferred to Central on 2 August 1965). Initially, closure was temporary with work taking place on the electrification of the main line to Bournemouth but, with services over the S&D ceasing in March 1966, it was decided that Central was capable of handling all passenger traffic to the town and West's closure became permanent. The station was subsequently demolished; the site is now occupied by a car park and A338 Wessex Way. The approaches to the station, however, survive, with the area occupied by Bournemouth EMU depot. *John McCann/Online Transport Archive*

On 15 September 1964 Ivatt-designed 2-6-2T No 41214 awaits departure at Bournemouth West with the 5.30pm service to Templecombe. When the station was originally opened it was provided with only two platforms; these were soon inadequate and the station was extended two years later with an additional four platforms. The platforms were initially numbered 1 to 6 from north to south; this numbering was, however, reversed on 30 September 1931. Facilities provided included a goods yard with a single road goods shed and carriage sidings. Bournemouth West was controlled by a signalbox located just to the west of the station throat; this was, however, converted into a ground frame on 1 November 1965 – shortly after the official closure of the station (on 4 October 1965) and the simultaneous withdrawal of freight facilities – before being closed completely on 5 September 1966. *Gavin Morrison*

The first station west of Evercreech Junction on the line towards Glastonbury & Street was Pylle, which was downgraded and renamed Pylle Halt from 4 November 1957. The station opened on 3 February 1862. Until 1929 there was a passing loop and the station was provided with two platforms; in that year, the loop was closed and the signalbox – located at the west end of the surviving Up platform – was downgraded to become a ground frame. This view, taken from the derelict platform in August 1962, shows the station viewed towards the west.
Les Folkard/Online Transport Archive

On 29 June 1962, Class 3F 0-6-0 No 43216 is seen heading from Pylle with a service to Highbridge. Freight facilities were withdrawn from Pylle on 10 June 1963 – but already look overgrown a year earlier – and the station closed completely on 7 March 1966. The main station building and goods shed are still extant – having been converted for residential use – but the road bridge, which carries the A37 Fosse Way, has been removed, blocking the trackbed. *Derek Cross*

The ex-S&D station at Wells – Priory Road – viewed from the north on 3 August 1951 shortly before it lost its passenger services (on 29 October 1951) with the closure of the branch line to Glastonbury & Street. The station's small goods yard – visible on the left-hand side of the photograph – remained in use, however, accessed via the ex-GWR line from Yatton to Witham. Services over the latter continued to pass through Priory Road station, which was latterly shorn of the overall roof shown in this view, without stopping until passenger services on that route ceased on 9 September 1963.

The S&D station was the first of three stations in Wells to open – on 15 March 1859 – with the opening of the line from Glastonbury. The future GWR route – comprising two broad gauge lines to Tucker Street and East – were only connected over S&D metals following conversion to standard gauge in the mid-1870s. Freight facilities at Priory Road were withdrawn on 13 July 1964. The station was subsequently demolished and the site incorporated within a road scheme.
Tony Wickens/Online Transport Archive

With the opening of the branch from Glastonbury to Wells, the Somerset Central Railway opened a small two-road stone-built engine shed at Wells. The structure is seen here, viewed from the east, on 3 August 1951, and shows the modified flat roof over the northern half of the building installed by the LMS, probably in the late 1930s. The shed was officially closed in 1947 but remained a stabling point thereafter until the closure of the Glastonbury branch three months after this photograph was taken. The shed was subsequently demolished.
Tony Wickens/Online Transport Archive

Viewed looking towards the east on 3 August 1951, the Wells branch train stands at the northern face of the island platform at Glastonbury & Street. The station, which gained its '& Street' suffix in 1885, originally opened on 28 August 1854. The station buildings, which were constructed in wood, included extensive platform canopies and an ornate footbridge (even though not all passengers seem to have taken advantage of the latter). When recorded here, the Wells branch was coming to the end of its life; services ceased – and the line closed completely – on 29 October 1951. The station boasted a large goods yard, including a private siding serving the local saw mills. Freight facilities were withdrawn at the same time as the station lost its passenger services in March 1966. The station remained in an increasingly derelict condition for more than a decade after closure but was subsequently demolished (although one of the platform canopies was transferred to become a shelter in the market car park); the site is now occupied by an industrial estate although, in a gesture to its history, the main gates comprise a pair of level crossing gates. *Tony Wickens/Online Transport Archive*

On 20 August 1960 the signalman has the token ready for the section eastwards towards Glastonbury & Street as the train approaches the box at Shapwick. The station at Shapwick, which opened on 28 August 1854, was relatively simple with a wooden main building on the westbound platform. The 17-lever signalbox dated to the early years of the 20th century when it had been rebuilt following a fire that had destroyed the station. In addition to the passenger station, Shapwick also had a small goods yard, although this closed on 10 June 1963. The station itself and box survived until the line's final closure. At this point the S&D ran parallel to the South Drain and, although the station itself has disappeared, the trackbed eastwards is now a public footpath. *James Harrold/Transport Treasury*

Pictured in the Up bay at Edington Junction station with the branch line service to Bridgwater is Class 3F 0-6-0 No 43216. The station was opened as Edington Road on 28 August 1854; it became Edington in 1864 and Edington Junction with the opening of the Bridgwater branch on 21 July 1890. Following the withdrawal of passenger services to Bridgwater, it became Edington Burtle on 30 November 1952; it retained this name until final closure came on 7 March 1966. The station was rationalised in 1956 – as part of the run down of the line from Evercreech Junction to Highbridge – when the Down platform was taken out of use and the signalbox closed. Freight facilities were withdrawn on 13 July 1964. Although the station itself has been demolished, the two-storey station house remains as a private residence.
R. W. A. Jones/Online Transport Archive

No 43216 is pictured again, this time at the branch terminus at Bridgwater North. This station acquired its 'North' suffix on 26 September 1949. Passenger services over the branch from Edington Junction ceased on 1 December 1952 with the line closing completely on 4 October 1954; however, a connection, installed during that year, enabled the ex-S&D goods yard to be served from the ex-GWR main line. The goods yard was out of use by March 1966 and the new connection was severed in January 1967. Until World War 1, there was a short – half-mile – branch from the goods yard to serve a quay on the River Perrett. The track on this line was not removed until World War 2. The site of the station is now occupied by a supermarket and retail park.
R. W. A. Jones/Online Transport Archive

The small station at Bason Bridge was located alongside the River Brue and immediately west of the level crossing with Church Road. To the east of the level crossing was the milk factory owned by Wilts United Dairies that was the major provider of traffic from the station. Pictured at the station is ex-S&D 0-6-0 No 44560 with the 'Southern Wanderer' special organised by the Southern Counties Touring Society on 28 March 1965. General freight traffic to Bason Bridge ceased on 10 June 1963 with passenger services ceasing in March 1966. However, the section of line from Highbridge to Bason Bridge remained open to cater for milk tanker traffic until this ceased on 2 October 1972. At the time of writing the single platform at Bason Bridge remained as did the trackbed to the west; to the east, however, the trackbed and milk factory have disappeared to be replaced by an industrial estate.
Roy Hobbs/Online Transport Archive

Viewed from the east in September 1965, 2-6-2T No 41249 is seen departing from Highbridge station with a service to Templecombe. The locomotive was completed at Crewe in November 1949 and, when recorded here, was a relatively recent addition to the locomotives allocated to duties on the S&D having been transferred from Exmouth Junction to Templecombe in June 1965. Briefly stored during January 1966, No 41249 was reinstated the following month to Templecombe but was withdrawn for a final time with the closure of the S&D route in March 1966.
Derek Cross

The view taken from the station footbridge at Highbridge looking towards the east on 28 March 1965 when the station was visited by the 'Southern Wanderer' special. Visible in the distance are Highbridge C box and the erstwhile S&D works. Following the official opening of the line from Highbridge To Glastonbury on 17 August 1854, timetabled services commenced on 28 August 1854; these were, until 3 February 1862, operated by the Bristol & Exeter Railway. The S&D station was provided with had five platform faces; the two through roads – platforms 4 and 5 – provided access to the line through to Burnham-on-Sea; this line crossed the ex-GWR main line on level immediately to the north of the station. The line through to Glastonbury and Evercreech Junction closed on 7 March 1966.
John Meredith/Online Transport Archive

Highbridge East C – known as Highbridge Loco prior to Nationalisation – was a 25-lever box that controlled access to the S&D works and to the engine shed; it is pictured here on 28 March 1965. It was one of three ex-S&D boxes at Highbridge in 1965; the other two – known as East A and East B after Nationalisation – were both closed on 16 May 1965 when freight traffic was withdrawn from Highbridge Wharves. At one stage a three-road carriage shed was situated immediately behind Highbridge Loco box. *John Meredith/Online Transport Archive*

Pictured inside the two-road shed at Highbridge on 28 March 1965 is ex-GWR 0-6-0 No 3218. Although the shed, which was situated within the S&D works complex, was constructed in 1862 as a four-road building, only two of the roads were used to accommodate locomotives; a third road was used historically for carriage cleaning and testing with the fourth road being without track. The shed officially closed on 11 May 1959 but, as seen here, was used for the stabling of locomotives through until the final closure of the line in 1966.

John Meredith/Online Transport Archive

With the engine shed in the background, the locomotive that had hauled the Southern Counties Touring Society special on 28 March 1965 – 0-6-0 No 44560 (appropriately one of the type that were built for use on the line and was originally S&D No 61 when new in 1922) – is seen reversing back towards the station having taken water, prior to working the train back towards Evercreech Junction. Apart from the engine shed and water tower, the facilities at Highbridge also included a 50ft 0in turntable. The buildings to the right of the water tower are part of those constructed by the S&D as its workshops; these were opened in 1862. However, the need to achieve economies during the increasingly competitive 1920s, when the railways faced the increasing threat of the internal combustion engine, led to the closure of the works in 1930. Almost six decades after the final closure of the S&D line, there is now virtually no trace that the line ever existed at this point. Although the ex-GWR station remains on the main line, the area once occupied by the S&D platforms and works has been redeveloped for housing and business purposes.
John Meredith/Online Transport Archive

On 28 April 1957 the RCTS (London Branch) organised the North Somerset rail tour. Amongst the lines visited during the course of the day was the section from Highbridge to Burnham-on-Sea, where the train was booked to be between 4.10pm and 4.20pm. Although No 3440 *City of Truro* was used for the bulk of the outward journey, two Ivatt-designed 2-26-2Ts – Nos 41202 and 41203 – were employed on the various branches visited in Somerset. The former, however, was used alone for the section from Highbridge to Burnham-on-Sea and the train is pictured here prior to departure on its return journey to Highbridge. The Burnham-on-Sea extension opened on 3 May 1858. By the date of the excursion, the station had lost its regular passenger services – on 29 October 1951 – although summer excursions had operated after that date. Freight facilities were withdrawn from the station on 20 May 1963 and the line from Highbridge was closed completely the same day.
Gerald Druce/Online Transport Archive